D1071666

WHEELS, WHEELS, and More Wheels
By Ed Radlauer
Photographs by Ruth and Ed Radlauer

FOREST HOUSE ™

FOREST HOUSE™

Printed and bound in the United States of America.

Published by Forest House Publishing Co., Inc,
P. O. Box 738
Lake Forest, Illinois 60045

ISBN 1-878363-36-0

Cataloging-in-Publication Data

Radlauer, Ed, 1921-
   Wheels, wheels, and more wheels / by Ed Radlauer. Photographs by Ruth
and Ed Radlauer.—
   p. cm.
Includes word list.
A bathtub on wheels leads children in an exploration of other vehicles with
wheels.
ISBN 1-878363-36-0
1. Wheels—Fiction   I. Radlauer, Ruth.   II. Title.
PZ7   [E]

Created By Radlauer Productions, Inc. for Forest House Publishing Co., Inc.

Ed Radlauer's

WHEELS, WHEELS, and More Wheels

Author/illustrator Ed Radlauer has been
attracting youngsters to the printed
page for over 20 years. Now the former
educator will continue that work with
the publication of the ED RADLAUER BOOKS.

Look! It's a bathtub on wheels.
Look again! There are little bathtub wheels
in the front, and big wheels in the back.
It's time to start up the bathtub
engine. Let's—

—go!

This model steam engine has wheels
in the front, middle, and back.
The small wheels are in the front and back.
The big wheels are in the middle.
It's time to start up the model steam engine.
Let's—

—go!

Let's go? No, we can't go.
A very old steam engine tractor
with lots of big old wheels
is too old to go. This tractor could be
one of the oldest tractors in the world.
    Show the old steam engine tractor
to a friend. Tell your friend,
"This steam engine tractor is too old
to go. It could be one of the oldest
tractors in the—

—world.''

Look! Each rider is on one wheel.
That means each rider is on a unicycle.
Here's something to think about.
Is a unicycle wheel in the front,
in the back, or in the—

—middle?

Look, here's another unicycle.
To make a unicycle go, you need
people power. Here's something
to think about. How do you
steer a people-power—

—unicycle?

What's this? It has three wheels,
so it must be a tricycle.
But this is a backward tricycle
going forward.

Show the tricycle to a friend.
Tell your friend, ''This is a people-power,
backward tricycle going—

—forward.''

Is this another backward tricycle?
No, this is a super custom chopper cycle
with two wheels in front and four wheels
in the back.
Show the super custom chopper
to a friend. Tell your friend,
"This tricycle has two wheels
in the front and four wheels
in the—

—back."

Here's a super custom tow truck
with custom wheels. It's a tow truck,
so we can call it a "dragging wagon."
Show the custom truck to a friend.
Tell your friend, "The custom tow truck
has custom wheels and it's called a—

—'dragging wagon.' ''

Look! What's this? It's Number 91,
a racing kart. If your kart wheels are slow,
you will lose. But if your racing kart wheels
are fast, very fast, you will—

—win.

Is that an old drag racing roadster?
Yes, it's an old drag racing roadster
with little wheels in the front
and big wheels in the back.
If your drag racing wheels are slow,
you will lose. But if your drag racing
roadster wheels are fast, you will—

—win.

Let's go way back in time.
Let's go way back to the year 1943.
In 1943, someone in Germany built this
military wagon.
The wagon was built
with an air-cooled engine.
The military wagon was the first
of the famous German car called,
the Volkswagen, now called the VW Beetle.
The volkswagen VW Beetle is one
of the most famous cars in the—

—world.

Look! A pink VW Beetle.
Is there a mouth? Is there a nose?
A moustache? An ear? A Beetle
with a mouth, ear, nose, and moustache
must be a "People Beetle."
Show this car to a friend.
Tell your friend, "It's a—

—'People Beetle.' ''

Look! It's Number 12 Monster Beetle
with big beautiful wheels. Let's go?
No go. Monster Beetle is only a model.
Show Monster Beetle to a friend.
Tell your friend, ''Number 12
Monster Beetle is only a—

—beautiful model."

Look! It's another four-wheel
VW Beetle car. Is it a beautiful car
with big wheels? No, it's an ugly car
with little ugly wheels. Maybe it's
the ugliest VW Beetle in the world.
Show this VW car
with little ugly wheels to a friend.
Tell your friend, "This VW car
may be the ugliest car in the—

—world.''

WHEELS

Word List

See how fast you can read the WHEELS word list.
See how fast a friend can read the WHEELS word list.

air-cooled engine	middle
backward	military wagon
bathtub	monster
beautiful	people-power
built	racing kart
custom wheels	steam
drag racing roadster	super custom chopper cycle
dragging wagon	super custom tow truck
engine	tractor
famous	tricycle
first	ugly
forward	unicycle
German	Volkswagen
Germany	VW Beetle
kart	world

All of these words are in this book.
See how many you can find.